WRITERS AND THEIR WORK NO. 52

Laurence Sterne

by D. W. JEFFERSON

Published for The British Council
and The National Book League
by Longmans, Green & Co.

Two shillings and sixpence net

Laurence Sterne (1713–68), the author of *Tristram Shandy* and *A Sentimental Journey through France and Italy*, is one of the greater English comic writers, the influence of whose style and methods is as evident to-day as it has ever been in literary history. 'Sterne's character', writes Mr. Jefferson, 'is of a kind which needs, but which also inspires, tender and careful handling.' His own essay is an excellent example of sympathetic interpretation.

Mr. Jefferson was educated at Leeds University and at Merton College, Oxford. He has been a member of the staff of the Department of English Literature at Leeds since 1935. He taught for some time during the war years at Fuad I University, Cairo. He has lectured on English Literature for the British Council in Egypt, Israel, Jordan, Sweden, and France.

Bibliographical Series
of Supplements to 'British Book News'
on Writers and Their Work

*

GENERAL EDITOR
Bonamy Dobrée

STERNE
*From a painting by an unidentified artist
in the National Portrait Gallery*

LAURENCE STERNE

by
D. W. JEFFERSON

PUBLISHED FOR
THE BRITISH COUNCIL
and the NATIONAL BOOK LEAGUE
by LONGMANS, GREEN & CO.

LONGMANS, GREEN & CO. LTD.
6 & 7 Clifford Street, London W.1
Thibault House, Thibault Square, Cape Town
605–611 Lonsdale Street, Melbourne, C.1

LONGMANS, GREEN & CO. INC.
119 West 40th Street, New York 18

LONGMANS, GREEN & CO.
20 Cranfield Road, Toronto 16

ORIENT LONGMANS PRIVATE LTD.
Calcutta   Bombay   Madras
Delhi   Hyderabad   Dacca

First published in 1954
Reprinted 1959

PR
3716
.J4

Printed in Great Britain by Unwin Brothers Limited
Woking and London

CONTENTS

LAURENCE STERNE *page* 7
A SELECT BIBLIOGRAPHY 33

¶ LAURENCE STERNE was born at Clonmel, Tipperary, Ireland, on 24 November 1713: he died in London on 8 March 1768.

LAURENCE STERNE

I

IN MORE than one place Laurence Sterne claims a medicinal value for his great comic masterpiece *Tristram Shandy*:

> —If 'tis wrote against anything,—'tis wrote, an' please your worships, against the spleen! in order, by a more frequent and a more convulsive elevation and depression of the diaphragm, and the succussations of the intercostal and abdominal muscles in laughter, to drive the *gall* and other *bitter juices* from the gall-bladder, liver, and sweet-bread of his majesty's subjects, with all the inimicitious passions which belong to them, down into their duodenums.

In another passage he writes:

> True Shandeism, think what you will against it, opens the heart and lungs, and like all those affections which partake of its nature, it forces the blood and other vital fluids of the body to run freely through its channels, makes the wheel of life run long and cheerfully round.

But turning from *Tristram Shandy* to a letter written to his amiable companion, John Hall-Stevenson, in which he complains of 'a thin death-doing pestiferous north-east wind' blowing upon him, we see the virtues of the Shandean philosophy in another light:

> ... and if God ... had not poured forth the spirit of Shandeism into me, which will not suffer me to think two minutes upon any grave subject, I would else just now lay down and die....

Sterne was long a sick man, a victim to hæmorrhages of the lungs, driven to travel abroad for his health. The gaiety of *Tristram Shandy* and also of *A Sentimental Journey* takes on a different significance against this background.

Sterne's character is of a kind which needs, but which also inspires, tender and careful handling. No reputation has suffered more than his from nineteenth-century moral prejudice and obtuseness: Thackeray's account of him in *The English Humorists of the Eighteenth Century* is one of the disgraces of English criticism. Our own age can perhaps more easily accept simply as psychological fact some aspects of his life which gave scandal to the Victorians. He was emotionally unstable. His marriage with Elizabeth Lumley was not very successful: she has been described as a 'fretful porcupine', and no doubt there were faults on his side. After eighteen years of married life she had a curious mental breakdown, and it was after this that Sterne's helpless susceptibility manifested itself in a series of sentimental relationships (they were not affairs of physical passion) which are not quite in keeping with the character of a clergyman. He was singularly unabashed about this side of his nature, as the following passage from a letter testifies:

> ... I am glad that you are in love—'twill cure you (at least) of the spleen, which has a bad effect on both man and woman—I myself must ever have some dulcinea in my head—it harmonizes the soul—and in those cases I first endeavour to make the lady believe so, or rather I begin first to make myself believe that I am in love—but I carry on my affairs quite in the French way, sentimentally—'*l'amour*' (they say) '*n'est rien sans sentiment*'.

What the modern reader may find engaging here is Sterne's easy candour. Perhaps it is easier to-day to sympathize with an aspect of him which has tended in the past to alienate sympathy; namely, the elements of artifice which accompanies his expressions of emotion. Even in the *Journal to Eliza*, written to the woman who meant much more to him than any of the others, and during a period of overwrought emotion combined with poor health, he shows an artist's awareness of the exquisite distress he is depicting:

> Ap. 28. I was not deceived, Eliza! by my presentiment that I should find thee out in my dreams; for I have been with thee almost the whole night, alternatively soothing Thee, or telling thee my sorrows—I have rose up comforted & strengthened,—& found myself so much better, that I ordered my Carriage, to carry me to our mutual friend—Tears ran down her cheeks when

she saw how pale & wan I was—never gentle creature sympathized more tenderly—I beseech you, cried the good Soul, not to regard either difficulties or expences, but to fly to Eliza directly —I see you will dye without her—save yourself for her—How shall I look her in the face? What can I say to her, when on her return I have to tell her, That her Yorick is no more!—Tell her my dear friend, said I, that I will meet her in a better world— & that I have left this, because I could not live without her; tell Eliza, my dear friend, added I—That I died broken hearted—and that you were a witness to it—as I said this she burst into the most pathetick flood of Tears that ever kindly Nature shed— you never beheld so affecting a scene—'twas too much for Nature! . . .

Upon our response to this depends very largely our response to Sterne as a man. To some readers it is sheer wanton indulgence, self-conscious manipulation of the feelings, and fundamentally insincere. But perhaps it is wiser to recognize that everyone has his 'style', in the emotions as in other things. To the present writer, at least, the *Journal to Eliza* is a moving document, the record of genuine suffering. If Sterne was, to use an unkind modern term, somewhat exhibitionist about his feelings, these outpourings with all their elements of conscious heightening are the expression of a need. There is, of course, pathological weakness here, and it must be related to his state of physical health. But it was Sterne's gift that he could make something out of his weaknesses. He expressed himself to the full, and somehow the result is humanly acceptable. Recent scholarship has uncovered some much less attractive cases of emotional instability among the Victorian writers; Thackeray himself was somewhat frustrated and unfulfilled, which may help to explain his dislike of Sterne's freedom and fluency in matters of the heart.

We might feel less kindly about this side of Sterne's life were it not for the agreeable impression we get from his letters and from outside testimony of his efforts during these later years to make things as comfortable as possible for his wife. The solicitous interest he took in the details of her journey to France when she decided to join him there with their daughter Lydia; his patience with her trying humours during their sojourn there; and his reasonable attitude to her financial demands, after he had returned to his Yorkshire parish and she had formed the project of living apart from him; all this testifies to good elements in him and to a sweetness of disposition in the face of vexation. How far he is to be blamed for the central fact of the failure of their marriage is a matter concerning which we have insufficient evidence.

Our own age is not only better equipped temperamentally to appreciate Sterne and his work; it also has the advantage of more information about his life, for which we are indebted partly to a nineteenth-century biographer, Percy Fitzgerald, but more especially to an American scholar, Wilbur L. Cross, whose monumental *Life and Times of Laurence Sterne* (1925) destroyed a number of malicious traditions which misled earlier critics. We now have more evidence, for example, about his treatment of his mother, whom he was alleged to have scandalously neglected. Sterne's father was a poor ensign who made an unfortunate marriage in Flanders with the daughter of a sutler: he appears to have married her because he owed money to her father. Born in 1713, Laurence spent his infancy in barracks in Ireland, and was then sent to school in Yorkshire, where he came under the protection of his father's relatives, upon whom he was dependent for the expenses of his education, his father dying penniless in 1731. During the period when Sterne was at Cambridge and for some years after his ordination as a clergyman in the Church of England, his mother lived in Ireland on her pension, supplemented by what she earned by keeping an embroidery school, and there appears to have been little contact between them. It was in 1741, when Sterne was established as a prebendary of York and married to a woman whom she believed to have money, that his mother conceived the policy of coming with her daughter to England to live at his expense. The story of the persecutions which he suffered over a period of years, of the drain upon his income and his various financial anxieties, of her unreasonableness and dishonesty and his repeated efforts not to forget that he was a son, 'though she forgot that she was a mother', is told in a letter by Sterne himself which was not published until 1892. We have only his word for its truth, but it is a circumstantial document and has the ring of genuineness. It was written in indignation to his uncle and old enemy, Dr. Jaques Sterne who, after playing a not very helpful part in this affair, had caused her to be placed in a charitable institution in York (according to some, 'the common gaol') apparently with no other motive than the wish to damage his nephew's reputation. Before the publication of this letter there were many, no doubt, who believed, with Byron, that Sterne 'preferred whining over a dead ass to relieving a living mother'. We do not know the whole story. It seems likely that Sterne's handling of this extremely difficult situation fell short of the heroic, but Cross's comment that 'a man of finer grain would have taken in his mother and sister and made the best of it', is a lapse into insensitive moralizing. Not that moral principles do not apply to Sterne as much as to other men, but one of the effects of his elusive and sympathetic personality upon us is to remind us of how little, even when we know the 'facts', we can judge any human being's response to the strains and stresses of life.

What can be said of his character as a clergyman? It is difficult for us to appreciate the motives with which, in this period, men like Swift and Sterne entered the Church: they seem to have had no special insight into their religion, no overmastering sense of vocation. Both of these clergymen had a distinctly secular turn of wit. Part of the answer is that in an age when intense religious fervour was condemned by reasonable people as 'enthusiasm', the tendency was for clergymen to behave outwardly as men of the world, so that it is not easy for us to tell how serious they were beneath the surface. Sterne's sermons have little doctrinal content, and show no feeling for the supernatural values of his religion; one has the impression that he takes all this for granted. It is the human moral aspects of the Bible stories that he dwells upon, often with sensitiveness and insight, though none of his sermons rises to great heights. As for his parochial activities, from the little evidence we have it is impossible to say how diligent he was. In a letter to the Archbishop of York in 1743 replying to a *questionnaire* he makes the remarkable statement: 'I Catechise every Sunday in my Church during Lent, But explain our Religion to the Children and Servants of my Parishioners in my House every Sunday Night during Lent, from six o'clock till nine', which, according to Canon Ollard, who published the letter (in *The Times Literary Supplement*, 18 March 1926) and examined many other such returns, stands alone as an example of zeal. Sometimes the evidence points to a more easy-going attitude. Cross quotes a story to the effect that as Sterne, 'was going over the fields on a Sunday to preach at Stillington, it happened that his pointer dog sprung a covey of partridges, when he went directly home for his gun and left his flock that was waiting for him in the church in the lurch'. On the whole Cross, whose knowledge of him is unrivalled, gives him a good character for attention to his ecclesiastical duties and generosity to his curates, a class of men who in that age were not always well treated.

For nearly thirty years his associations were with York and the villages north of it: Sutton-in-the-Forest, Stillington, and finally Coxwold, the living of which he obtained in 1760. Like other parsons of his day he farmed his own land, and it is not altogether agreeable to note that he used the practice of enclosure to build up a sizeable property. That Sterne was attached in this way to his locality, with a countryman's feeling for it, is one of the things which contribute to the flavour of *Tristram Shandy*; and a love for Coxwold, his 'land of plenty' and 'delicious retreat', colours the pages of the *Journal to Eliza*, written in his last year. But in the last eight years of his life he was absent for long periods, partly because of bad health and the need to travel, partly because as a man of letters he was eagerly claimed by the society of the metropolis.

He had an unholy taste for the company of Rabelaisian wits, like John Hall-Stevenson who entertained his club of 'Demoniacs' at Skelton Castle ('Crazy Castle' as he called it), which was near enough for Sterne to pay frequent visits. In the days of his fame the freedom of his conversation gave offence to Dr. Johnson, who felt the disgrace to the cloth. *A propos* of Johnson's disapproval, it is quite likely that Sterne's anarchic wit, stimulated by an uncontrolled eagerness of temperament, often went too far, so that he gave an unjust impression of his true worth.

Sterne developed late as a literary artist. His earliest writings, as far as we know, were political articles and letters written for local newspapers during a celebrated Yorkshire election of 1741. It was as an assistant to his uncle, Jaques Sterne, who was a vigorous Whig and persecutor of Catholics and Jacobites, that he had this short spell as a political propagandist, but later he regretted it as 'dirty work', and his refusal to write any more in such a cause earned him the undying ill-will of Dr. Sterne, manifested, as we have seen, in the situation created by his mother. Apart from the occasional sermon which was printed he wrote nothing more for nearly twenty years.[1] In 1759 a local squabble about ecclesiastical preferments provoked him to compose a witty allegory in the manner of Swift entitled *A Political Romance*, later known as *The History of a Good Warm Watch-Coat*. About New Year 1760 he published the first two volumes of *Tristram Shandy*. At the age of forty-six then Sterne, hitherto quite obscure, suddenly achieved a celebrity to which there can be few parallels in literary history.

[1] Unless some literary articles in the *York Journal* of 1750–1, referred to by Dr. L. P. Curtis in his *Sterne's Politicks*, are by him, but we have no definite evidence.

Visiting London by chance a few months after *Tristram Shandy* made its *début*, he discovered that copies of it 'could not be had either for love or money'; and the news that the author was in town led to an astonishing sequence of social triumphs. Lord Rockingham, one of the great Yorkshire Whigs and a future Prime Minister, took the lead in welcoming him into the world of fashion; he made the acquaintance of the Duke of York; and he dined at Windsor, on the occasion of the installation of Prince Ferdinand of Brunswick as Knight of the Garter. Among his new friends in the world of the arts was David Garrick. Those who are not well-disposed towards Sterne may be inclined to regard this as a somewhat meretricious social success: he was an amusing companion and a fashionable novelty; but this is not the whole truth. Dr. John Hill (a dubious figure, but there is no reason to question his good faith here) wrote in a current periodical: 'Everybody is curious to see the author; and, when they see him, every body loves the man; there is a pleasantry in his conversation that always pleases; and a goodness in his heart, which adds the greater tribute of esteem.'

Further volumes of *Tristram Shandy* appeared over the next seven years, the pace of composition being greatly reduced by periods of illness and the distractions of travel abroad. On his first journey to France in 1762–4 he was given a most flattering reception into Parisian society, and became an associate of the Holbach circle. It is with his second visit to the Continent in 1765–6 that *A Sentimental Journey* appears to be mainly concerned, though some incidents from the earlier visit are incorporated; but after all it is not primarily as a factual record that we value this remarkable work of art, which was published in 1768, a few weeks before his death.

One of the more damaging of the legends which recent biographers have been able to correct concerns his death. It is not true that he died friendless and in mean lodgings. His last days were spent in comfortable apartments where he was much visited until he was too ill—he died of pleurisy—to receive any more, and there were friends to show him kindness until the end. It is true, however, that he left large debts, the sale of his works, though considerable, being insufficient to offset the expenses of foreign travel and of a separate establishment for his wife and daughter.

II

Tristram Shandy is one of those works to which one can return again and again with increasing satisfaction, but let us begin by looking at it as it appears to the delighted but baffled reader who is approaching it for the first time. His impression is of a kind of rich chaos, an inspired disorder. First, there is the apparent lack of progression. The reader waits helplessly until somewhere in the third book for the hero to be born; the christening occurs in the fourth; in the sixth there is talk of putting him into breeches; and this, apart from a freakish, wholly unrelated passage about his travels in the seventh, is as far as his history is developed. Whatever the reader is getting, it is not what the title promised: the 'Life and Opinions' of the hero. Meanwhile, there are *digressions*. No writer, it is safe to say, ever used the digression more often or, it would seem, more wantonly. It would be difficult to find digressions at a steeper angle from the main course than some of Sterne's. Yet Sterne is completely at home and at his ease amidst this seeming anarchy; and if the reader loses all sense of movement and direction, something sustains him: an atmosphere so humanly satisfying and beguiling that the author, with all his vagaries, has him totally at his mercy.

Lying on the surface of *Tristram Shandy* are innumerable little manifestations of Sterne's playfulness and delight in absurdity, which serve to accentuate the impression of artistic irresponsibility. For example, half-way through the third book, when Mr. Shandy falls asleep as he sits in the parlour waiting for his son to be born, and Uncle Toby follows him, and the other characters have also been conveniently disposed of for the time being, the narrator now decides that he has a moment or two to spare, so he writes his Preface! When the moment arrives in the sixth book for a picture of the Widow Wadman, the narrator abdicates and invites the reader to supply it himself ('Sit down, Sir, paint her to your own mind—as like your mistress as you can—as unlike your wife as your conscience will let you—'), leaving a blank page for the purpose. And in the last book, when Uncle Toby is about to call on the Widow Wadman to pay court to her, and is in fact on the threshold, the chapter ends and the next two chapters (numbers 18 and 19) are left blank, to be supplied out of their order a few pages later. After the sketch of parson Yorick in the first book—a Cervantic self-portrait, full of humour and of Sterne's peculiar brand of pathos—a page is devoted to his tombstone. At the end of the sixth book, affecting to mend his ways and tell his story 'in a tolerable strait line', he draws a number of irregular lines representing the tortuous paths taken in the earlier books. And if the reader, turning over the page from Book IV, Ch. xxiii, thinks that something has gone wrong at the printer's, he will soon see that it is just another of the author's jokes: there is no twenty-fourth chapter, and there is a gap in the pagination signifying the loss of ten pages.

But some readers will see, even on their first approach, that there is a good deal of method in Sterne's chaos. There is, for example, quite a good reason why the hero's birth should be so long delayed: it is not a beginning, it is a climax. The novel opens with his begetting, and no one can complain of lack of promptness in the treatment of it. In most autobiographical novels the birth and infancy of the hero are passed over fairly quickly, the main interest being attached to his later adventures; but Sterne's novel is different. Its theme, to reduce it to a simple formula, is 'How the hero came into the world and how, owing to various mishaps pre-natal and post-natal, he came to be the unfortunate creature he is'. It is as if a modern novelist wrote a Freudian romance dealing with the decisive traumatic experiences of the central character: as in *Tristram Shandy*, it would not be necessary to trace the hero's career beyond infancy. It is part of Sterne's comic purpose that we should be somewhat befogged as to his intention, yet from the beginning there are plenty of explicit indications as to what he is doing. His technique is to dangle the point in front of the reader's nose, but also to keep him so much entertained and bewildered by other things that he will probably not see it. The present writer could not have identified the central plan of *Tristram Shandy* after the first reading, but there is no reason why an observant reader should not do so.

The first chapter begins with these words:

> I wish either my father or my mother, or indeed both of them, as they were in duty both equally bound to it, had minded what they were about when they begot me. . . .

And then follows a discourse on 'the animal spirits, as how they are transferred from father to son etc. etc.' and how much depends on their condition during this important journey; and we are told of the ill-timed question of his mother ('Pray, my dear, have you not forgot to wind up the clock?'—an example of Locke's doctrine of association of ideas, in which Sterne was much interested) which, by interrupting Mr. Shandy, 'scattered and dispersed the animal spirits, whose business it was to have escorted and gone hand in hand with the HOMUNCULUS, and conducted him safe to the place destined for his reception'. This is the first of the series of catastrophes blighting the fortunes of the infant hero.

The second arises out of a clause in Mrs. Shandy's marriage settlement, the sense of which is that if she becomes pregnant her husband undertakes to pay the expenses of her journey to and confinement in London; but if on any occasion she puts him to this expense 'upon false cries and tokens', she forfeits these rights the next time. Unluckily for the young hero a fruitless journey to London was made in the year before his birth, under peculiarly annoying circumstances for Mr. Shandy, as it was towards the end of September, 'when his wall-fruit and green-gages especially, in which he was very curious, were just ready for pulling'. The terms are enforced, it is settled that the hero shall be born in the country, and 'I was doom'd, by marriage articles, to have my nose squeez'd as flat to my face, as if the destinies had spun me without one'; but this is looking ahead.

Mr. Shandy is a man of theories, and he applies his speculative mind to the supreme parental task of ensuring that his child shall have the best start in life. One of his beliefs concerns noses; namely, that 'the excellency of the nose is in a direct arithmetical proportion to the excellency of the wearer's fancy'. The events culminating in Tristram's being brought into the world defective in this respect have therefore to be traced with some care; and, indeed, the narrator lavishes every circumstantial embellishment upon the various stages of the fatal sequence. In the first place, Mrs. Shandy is as obstinate in her own way as her husband: deprived of the best professional attention she insists on having the most primitive, the local old woman, in preference to Dr. Slop, an operator with an impressive equipment of obstetric instruments. So, by way of compromise, she gets her own way, while Dr. Slop is to sit in the parlour and drink a bottle of wine with Mr. Shandy and Uncle Toby, for which he is to receive a fee of five guineas. But as they sit there Dr. Slop is called upon, in an emergency, to intervene: the old woman has fallen on the edge of the fender and bruised her hip; and he too has suffered a somewhat Shandean misadventure, having cut his thumb while trying to sever the knots in the strings with which Obadiah, the servant at Shandy Hall, has tied up his bag of instruments. The next thing we hear of Dr. Slop, after he has been suddenly summoned imperfectly prepared to his task, is that, having applied his 'vile instruments' with disastrous effect, he is making 'a bridge for master's nose . . . with a piece of cotton and a thin piece of whalebone out of Susannah's stays'.

The dismal climax is led up to with touches of dramatic heightening. 'Truce!—truce, good Dr. Slop: stay thy obstetrick hand. . . .' Thus begins an eloquent invocation to the operator as he approaches Shandy Hall. 'Sport of small accidents, Tristram Shandy! that thou art, and ever will be!' are the bitter words provoked by Obadiah's tying of the knots.

Such is the story of the hero's birth, when the relevant details are abstracted and pieced together; but how unlike the effect of the novel, in which the fragments of the narrative have the appearance of interruptions to digressions!

One of Sterne's notable characteristics is an imaginative interest in the physiological aspects of human situations. It is no accident that the Shandean philosophy, stated on the first page of this essay, should be expressed in physiological terms. An excursion into the history of science would be necessary to explain why it was possible for Sterne and his predecessors, Rabelais and Burton, to derive so much inspiration from a subject which in modern times has not had much to give to the literary artist. The fact is that the old speculative approach to knowledge, the pre-scientific approach, offered greater opportunities to the imagination, especially in the direction of comic travesty, than the specialized experimental disciplines of later periods. Mr. Shandy with his doctrine of noses and other curious excursions into physiological theory, is a speculative philosopher of the old school. And in becoming more efficient, science has acquired a sterilized quality: the fusion of scientific ideas with a homely personal manner or a lively fancy has gone. There are certain passages in *Tristram Shandy*—for example, the last chapter of Book II, in which Mr. Shandy's mind, running on obstetrics, is excited by the advantages of the Cæsarian section (he mentions it to his wife 'merely as a matter of fact; but seeing her turn pale as ashes' drops the subject), and the later chapters of Book III, in which he goes deeply into the philosophy of noses—where his curious pedantry takes on an extraordinary richness of flavour, a flavour to which we are accustomed in Rabelais, who was immensely learned in medicine and imaginatively alive to the poetry of the bodily functions. Here, for example, is a passage dealing with the ideas of Ambrose Paroeus 'chief surgeon and nose-mender to Francis the ninth of France'. His view is

> . . . that the length and goodness of the nose was owing simply to the softness and flaccidity of the nurse's breast—as the flatness and shortness of *puisne* noses was to the firmness and elastic repulsion of the same organ of nutrition in the hale and lively—which, tho happy for the woman, was the undoing of the child, inasmuch as his nose was so snubb'd, so rebuff'd, so rebated, and so refrigerated thereby, as never to arrive *ad mensuram suam legitimam*;—but that in case of the flaccidity and softness of the nurse or mother's breast—by sinking into it, quoth Paroeus, as into so much butter, the nose is comforted, nourish'd, plump'd up, refresh'd, refocillated, and set a growing for ever.

The delight in strange words, and the play between learned and homely words, gives a piquancy to the diction reminiscent of the older writers to whom Sterne was indebted.

The atmosphere in which the drama of the hero's birth is enacted is charged, then, with obsessions: obsessions with obstetrics, with noses, and also with names. Thwarted over his son's nose Mr. Shandy turns to his theory that a name has an important positive or negative influence on its owner's destiny. If his son can be christened Trismegistus he may still enter upon life handsomely endowed. But the child has a fit, the christening has to be conducted in a hurry, and while his father, who has been roused from his bed, looks round for his breeches, the name has been irretrievably reduced to Tristram, a name which ranks very low in Mr. Shandy's system. He is still not wholly discouraged in his attempts to apply his learning to the problems of parenthood: he composes a *Tristra-paedia*, a plan for Tristram's education, on the lines of Xenophon's *Cyropaedia*; he develops a curious theory about physical health; he discovers a short cut to knowledge based on the use of auxiliary verbs.

It is one of Sterne's structural devices to interrupt the history of the hero's birth by filling in the human background, so that the Shandy world is well peopled and familiar to us when the moment for his arrival comes. He preferred to do this in digressions, though if he had wished he could have contrived a more orthodox framework. Because the hero is not yet born these sections have the appearance of being deviations from the matter in hand and, as we have seen, it is part of Sterne's purpose that the reader should never know quite where he is. Thus several chapters in the first book are devoted to Yorick, a digression the pretext for which is rather slender: he comes in *à propos* of the old midwife to whom he used to lend his horse. And there is a sequence of chapters about Uncle Toby, with an elaborate explanation of the origin of his 'hobby-horse'. In an extremely interesting chapter (Bk. I, xxii) Sterne claims—playfully but there is serious truth in it—that his work is digressive and progressive at the same time. The digression often has a central purpose, though it also has its independent life. There are some digressions in *Tristram Shandy* for which this excuse could hardly be offered. There is something to be said for the view that freedom to digress is an artistic advantage, provided that the writer can control the tension set up between new sources of interest and the reader's anxiety to reach a promised goal; and ability to manipulate the reader in this way is certainly one of Sterne's gifts. His lyrical defence of digressions is worth remembering:

> Digressions, incontestably, are the sunshine;—they are the life, the soul of reading!—take them out of this book, for instance,—you might as well take the book along with them;—one cold

eternal winter would reign on every page of it; restore them to the writer;—he steps forth like a bridgegroom,—bids All-hail; brings in variety, and forbids the appetite to fail.

There is another reason for his use of digressions. One of the features of the Shandy world is the intensity with which the characters are absorbed in their own ideas and fantasies. Both Mr. Shandy and Uncle Toby are, to use Sterne's expression, 'hobby-horsical', and Sterne's greatness as an artist is nowhere more manifest than in his ability to give imaginative depth to their preoccupations; otherwise what would be more boring than Mr. Shandy's theories or more childish than Uncle Toby's toy fortifications? The two brothers, though continually together and full of brotherly affection, virtually inhabit different mental spheres, which collide sometimes though they can hardly be said to meet. Uncle Toby's 'hobby-horse' has its origin in his attempts, while he is recovering from his wound obtained at the siege of Namur, to explain to visitors how it all happened. The complexity of the terrain confuses him, and the story breaks down, so in order to clarify it he resorts to military maps and textbooks, until his servant, Corporal Trim, has the inspired idea of building miniature fortifications on the bowling green, where they fight mock battles with improvised field-pieces made from such materials as a melted down pewter shaving basin and the leads from sash-windows. As Mr. Shandy expounds his philosophical views Uncle Toby, smoking quietly in his corner and comprehending little, makes remarks of engaging simplicity; but when his brother speaks of a train of ideas, his mind turns readily to a train of artillery, and when it is reported that Dr. Slop is making a bridge he is very gratified, thinking of the broken drawbridge on the bowling-green which has given him some trouble; and the history of the drawbridge provides us with a digression at this point. Sterne enjoyed furnishing illustrations for Locke's theory of association of ideas. More perhaps than any other novelist before Virginia Woolf, who may have learnt from him, he succeeds in capturing the atmosphere that is created when two or three people, ostensibly in conversation together, are in fact thinking their own thoughts and maintaining a rather tenuous contact with each other. 'I wish, Dr. Slop, you had seen what prodigious armies we had in Flanders', is Uncle Toby's contribution to a conversation specifically directed towards obstetrics.

Sterne is nowhere greater than in his power to convey a sense of Uncle Toby's absorption in his own private world, of its remoteness and of the completeness of the spell. It is when he takes us into that world, more than at any other time, that he shows us what he has learnt from Cervantes, to whom he continually makes affectionate references. Just as the Don's delusions are given a potency which challenges everyday reality, so that in each episode we see the events from two points of view, so Uncle Toby's curious game of make-believe is given an extraordinary inwardness. In certain passages describing his technical problems we visualize the objects as the toys they are, yet they are invested with some of the importance of the things they represent. The effect depends on the use of detail. One of Sterne's most pleasing artistic habits is that of entering delightedly into the particulars of a complicated situation: the details are felt, made real to the imagination. The following passage about the drawbridge has something of this quality:

> It turned it seems upon hinges at both ends of it, opening in the middle, one half of which turning to one side of the fosse, and the other to the other; the advantage of which was this, that by dividing the weight of the bridge into two equal portions, it impowered by uncle *Toby* to raise it up or let it down with the end of his crutch, and with one hand, which, as his garrison was weak, was as much as he could well spare—but the disadvantages of such a construction were insurmountable;——for by this means, he would say, I leave one half of my bridge in my enemy's possession——and pray of what use is the other?

Although the element of the fantastic is generously developed in the Shandy brothers, it is characteristic of Sterne's art that the better we come to know them the more they are seen to have of everyday human nature. The Shandy world is very solidly built, in spite of the magic elements in the atmosphere; whereas, for example, the best things in Dickens are entirely magical. Uncle Toby is a more real person than the great Dickens creations. He is of Shakespearian quality. Sterne can afford, in his half playful, half tender way, to give him an almost ideal charm: there are sufficient touches of plain, earthy normality to prevent the effect from being spoilt. We can believe completely in Uncle Toby, whereas it is necessary with Mr. Pickwick not to probe too far: we need to forget, for example, that he was once a business man.

A number of passages concerning Uncle Toby have always caught the fancy of Sterne's readers; for example, the too-often quoted story of the fly whom he allowed to escape: 'Go, says he, lifting up the sash, and opening his hand as he spoke, to let it escape;—go, poor devil, get thee gone, why should I hurt thee?—This world surely is wide enough to hold both thee and me.' Some of these episodes are composed rather in the manner of set pieces, an element of humorous artifice leaving the reader a certain amount of 'play' between different possible levels of emotional response. The following admirable passage occurs in the story of the poor dying soldier Le Fever upon whom Uncle Toby and Trim lavished their generous care:

——In a fortnight or three weeks, added my uncle *Toby*, smiling,—he might march.——He will never march; an' please your honour, in this world, said the corporal:——He will march; said my uncle *Toby*, rising up, from the side of the bed, with one shoe off:——An' please your honour, said the corporal, he will never march but to his grave:——He shall march, cried my uncle *Toby*, marching the foot which had a shoe on, though without advancing an inch,—he shall march to his regiment.—— He cannot stand it, said the corporal;——He shall be supported, said my uncle *Toby*;——He'll drop at last, said the corporal, and what will become of his boy?——He shall not drop, said my uncle *Toby*, firmly.——A-well-'o-day,—do what we can for him, said *Trim*, maintaining his point,—the poor soul will die:——He shall not die, by G—, cried my uncle *Toby*.

—The ACCUSING SPIRIT, which flew up to heaven's chancery with the oath, blush'd as he gave it in;—and the RECORDING ANGEL, as he wrote it down, dropp'd a tear upon the word, and blotted it out for ever.

III

Sterne is a figure of European importance, but mainly as the author of *A Sentimental Journey*. The influence of this work was prodigious: volumes have been written on its vogue in France, in Germany, in Italy; and countless publications with the word 'sentimental' in the title appeared during the generation or so after his death. It was from outside England, from such writers as Goethe and Heine, that the highest tributes to his genius came.

If the Victorians misread him ungenerously, disliking his vein of sentiment, he was certainly misread in the opposite way by some of his admirers outside England. Heine attributes to him a kind of intensity that is not his: 'He was the darling of the pale, tragic goddess. Once in an access of fierce tenderness, she kissed his young heart with such power, passion, and madness, that his heart began to bleed and suddenly understood all the sorrows of this world, and was filled with infinite compassion.' Those who know Sterne will know what kind of weight—not too much nor too little—to attach to such words as the following, which occur in a letter: 'I told you my design in it [i.e. *A Sentimental Journey*] was to teach us to love the world and our fellow creatures better than we do. . . .' To extract too much moral value from Sterne's work, on the authority of sentences such as these, may do him a disservice by provoking the old objection that the sentiment he helped to make fashionable is largely of the self-indulgent and self-deceiving kind. The disservice lies in the fact that Sterne's art, properly understood, forestalls this criticism. He had more wareness of the nature of emotional self-indulgence and self-deception than most of his critics. He showed just the right degree of awareness of them in himself: to have shown more would have been a fault.

Sterne seems to have played a decisive part in helping to establish certain meanings of the word 'sentimental' in English. There has been some debate as to whether the letter of about 1739-40 to his future wife in which the word occurs, seemingly for the first time, is authentic or not. The same passage with small verbal changes is found in the *Journal to Eliza* of nearly thirty years later, which means that either Sterne touched up an old letter or his daughter Lydia, in editing the letters, fabricated one out of materials from the then unpublished *Journal*. From what we know of Lydia's editorial morals, the latter seems highly likely; and this solution becomes doubly acceptable when we consider the history of the word. The passage runs: 'I gave a thousand pensive, penetrating looks at the chair thou hadst so often graced, in those quiet and sentimental repasts.' It has been shown that this meaning of the word ('tender', 'full of emotion') does not come into vogue until the 1760's, and then mainly through the writings of Sterne himself, the earlier meanings being based on the definition of 'sentiment' as 'thought' or 'moral reflection' rather than 'feeling'. Sterne, it is suggested, was influenced by the French meaning of 'sentiment' and was responsible for attaching it to the English word 'sentimental'.

Chilly generalizations concerning Sterne's place in contemporary literary history as an instrument in the creation of a vogue, have little bearing on the essential value or interest for us of *A Sentimental Journey*. It is very much a personal achievement, a miracle not to be repeated, though there were many attempts to imitate it. It is alive and significant for us while the fashions of the period seem peculiarly dead and unreal.

To appreciate *A Sentimental Journey* we must first accept the personality of the narrator. Sterne was supremely skilled in presenting himself to the reader, a matter requiring considerable tact and the right combination of naturalness and sophistication. From the outset we see him as a somewhat slender, though engaging personality. He is sympathetically responsive, but the situations described are such as to exercise the sympathies agreeably rather than otherwise. From the *Journal to Eliza*, a more personal document, we know that he was capable of more poignant feelings, but this is not the side of his nature which he reveals here. Perhaps the most important need for us in approaching the pathetic passages is to see them in their right proportion. The most usual way of misreading them is to assume that they claim more than they do, and then to attack them for their inadequacy. It is quite permissible, quite within the range of the author's intention, that in the chapter of 'The Dead Ass', for instance, we should note his fond cherishing of the little details of the story, and see in it an element of amiable affectation:

> Everybody who stood about, heard the poor fellow with concern——La Fleur offer'd him money.——The mourner said, he did not want it—it was not the value of the ass,—but the loss of him.—The ass, he said, he was assured loved him—and upon this told them a long story of a mischance upon their passage over the Pyrenean mountains, which had separated them from each other three days; during which time the ass had sought for him as much as he had sought the ass, and that they had neither scarce eat or drank till they met.
>
> Thou hast one comfort, friend, said I, at least, in the loss of thy poor beast; I'm sure thou hast been a merciful master to him.——Alas! said the mourner, I thought so, when he was alive—but now that he is dead, I think otherwise.——I fear the weight of myself and my afflictions together have been too much for him—they have shortened the poor creature's days, and I fear I have them to answer for.—Shame on the world! said I to myself—Did we love each other, as this poor soul but loved his ass—'twould be something.——

In a number of incidents he allows us to see the limits or

fluctuations of his generous feelings. When the Franciscan calls on him to beg for his convent, an inexplicable perversity prompts him to give nothing, in spite of—or because of?—the altruistic after-dinner mood in which he has been interrupted. (But later they are charmingly reconciled.) And what becomes of the caged starling, the plight of which provokes him to such an elaborate outburst on liberty? In the episode of the beggars he makes admirable play with the illusions which accompany charitable giving. On the strength of eight sous, which he has arbitrarily decided is all he has for this purpose, how much moral satisfaction he extracts from the scene which follows! How he delights in the refinements of courtesy with which the beggars accept what he gives! But when he realizes that he has given away 'his last sou', and that a *pauvre honteux* must go without, 'Good God! said I—and have I not one single sou to give him—But you have a thousand! cried all the powers of nature, stirring within me....'

In the following passage Sterne shows a humorous awareness of the absurdity of an infatuation, without robbing it of its charm:

> Then I will meet thee, said I, fair spirit, at Brussels—'tis only returning from Italy through Germany to Holland, by the rout of Flanders, home—'twill scarce be ten posts out of my way; but were it ten thousand! with what a moral delight will it crown my journey, in sharing in the sickening incidents of a tale of misery told to me by such a sufferer? to see her weep! and though I cannot dry up the fountain of her tears, what an exquisite sensation is there still left, in wiping them away from off the cheeks of the first and fairest of women, as I'm sitting with my handkerchief in my hand in silence the whole night beside her.

It is surprising that he has not been more valued for these corrective effects. There are two kinds of sophistication in him which our age might well find enjoyable: his recognition of foibles and vanities in the sphere of the affections and sympathies, and his uninhibited expression of the latter, notwithstanding this recognition.

How are we to take those episodes dealing with encounters with women? They are, as sexual adventures, rather slender: that he was not more passionate is, for some readers, a point against him. For other readers, the point against him is the philandering in itself. For others again it is his lingering over the details, his cherishing of each vibration. If we like Sterne, what will please us in these incidents is their fragrance, which this lingering over the details never spoils, and his gaiety of conscience. The fact is that for him such experiences are good. A point which needs to be made is that Sterne really believes in 'virtue', though he cannot resist a woman's charm, and the sweetness of the episodes in question lies in the amount he gets out of them without actual transgression. In 'The Conquest' he conveys admirably a fact of experience which is normal enough; namely, that it can be pleasant to feel desire and also pleasant not to give full rein to it. After he has refrained from laying hands on the *fille de chambre*, and has raised her up by the hand, led her out of the room, locked the door and put the key in his pocket, *then*, 'the victory being quite decisive', he kisses her on the cheek and takes her safe to the gate of the hotel. In the episode of the girl in the bookshop there is as much subtle suspense and intimacy of atmosphere as if it had been the beginning of an amorous intrigue:

> We stood still at the corner of the Rue de Nevers whilst this pass'd—We then stopp'd a moment whilst she disposed of her *Egarements de Coeur*, etc. more commodiously than carrying them in her hand—they were two volumes; so I held the second for her, whilst she put the first into her pocket; and then she held her pocket, and I put in the other after it.
>
> 'Tis sweet to feel by what fine-spun threads our affections are drawn together.
>
> We set off afresh, and as she took her third step, the girl put her hand within my arm—I was just bidding her—but she did it of herself with that undeliberating simplicity, which shew'd it was out of her head that she had never seen me before. For my part, I felt the conviction of consanguinity so strongly, that I

could not help turning half round to look in her face, and see if I could trace out any thing in it of a family likeness—Tut! said I, are we not all relations?

When we arrived at the turning up of the Rue de Gueneguault, I stopp'd to bid her adieu for good and all: the girl would thank me again for my company and kindess—She bid me adieu twice—I repeated it as often; and so cordial was the parting between us, that had it happen'd anywhere else, I'm not sure but I should have sign'd it with a kiss of charity, as warm and holy as an apostle.

But in Paris, as none kiss each other but the men—I did, what amounted to the same thing—

—I bid God bless her.

The delicacy of his narrative technique in episodes like these is one of his important contributions to the art of the novel. And with what piquancy and wit he describes the participants! Here is his description of Madame de L——, the object of his fantasies in the early chapters of the book:

When the heart flies out before the understanding, it saves the judgment a world of pains—I was certain she was of a better order of beings—however, I thought no more of her, but went on and wrote my preface.

The impression returned, upon my encounter with her in the street; a guarded frankness with which she gave me her hand, shewed, I thought, her good education and her good sense; and as I led her on, I felt a pleasurable ductility about her, which spread a calmness over all my spirits—

Good God! how a man might lead such a creature as this round the world with him! . . .

When we had got to the door of the Remise, she withdrew her hand from across her forehead . . . it was a face of about six and twenty—of a clear transparent brown, simply set off without rouge or powder—it was not critically handsome, but there was that in it, which in the frame of mind I was in, attached me more to it—it was interesting; I fancied it wore the characters of a widow'd look, and in that state of its declension, which had passed the two first paroxysms of sorrow, and was quietly beginning to reconcile itself to its loss. . . .

All these effects in Sterne may be examined in terms of technique in the handling of prose. Of all English novelists none had greater virtuosity in this respect. Sir Herbert Read, in an excellent introduction to *A Sentimental Journey*, has called attention to his range of styles, from the easy conversational manner of the opening chapter to the studied beauty of his description of 'The Captive', in the starling episode. It would be possible, taking his work as a whole, to identify a considerable number of ways in which prose is exploited to give to particular types of passage their essential flavour and tone. He is highly individual, but with all his idiosyncrasies he has the great eighteenth-century virtues: order, proportion, and a regard for fineness of surface.

While *A Sentimental Journey* has the virtues of a novel, it is, with much allowance made for embellishment, an account of incidents which really occurred and people whom he really met. Monsieur Dessein, the Calais hotel-keeper, made his fortune out of his appearance in Sterne's masterpiece; the Franciscan turns up some years later in Mrs. Piozzi's *Journey Through France*; rumour was active concerning the identity of Madame de L——. An absorbing interest in people, in all kinds of people, high and low, gives that quality to his work which, in the man himself, was perhaps the chief reason why he was so much sought after. That it should have been composed when he was in desperate health shows that, whatever his philosophy of life amounted to, it was not altogether a vain one.

LAURENCE STERNE

A Select Bibliography

(Place of publication London, unless stated otherwise)

Bibliography, etc.:

LIFE AND TIMES, by W. L. Cross. Third edition, revised. New Haven (1929).
Includes a detailed bibliography.

CATALOGUE OF STERNE'S LIBRARY, Edited by C. Wibley (1930).
A facsimile of the rare sale catalogue of Sterne's books.

A LIST OF CRITICAL STUDIES, 1896–1946. Edited by E. Cardasco. Brooklyn (1948).

NOTES ON THE EARLY EDITIONS OF 'TRISTRAM SHANDY', by J. M. Yoklavich in *Pub. Mod. Lang. Ass.* LXIII (1948).

ON COLLECTING STERNE, by J. C. T. Oates in *The Book Collector*, Winter 1952.

Collected Editions:

THE SERMONS OF MR. YORICK, 7 vols. (1760–9).
There were various eighteenth-century reprints in 2 and 6 vols.

WORKS, 5 vols. (1773–4).
The first collected edition. There were numerous eighteenth-century collections in 5, 7, 8, and 10 vols.

WORKS (1869).
The Globe edition.

WORKS, Edited by G. Saintsbury. 6 vols. (1894).

WORKS, Edited by W. L. Cross. 12 vols. New York (1904).

WORKS, 7 vols. Oxford (1926–7).
The Shakespeare Head Press edition.

Letters:

LETTERS FROM YORICK TO ELIZA (1775).

LETTERS TO HIS FRIENDS (1775).

LETTERS OF THE LATE MR. LAURENCE STERNE, 3 vols. (1775).

SEVEN LETTERS, Edited by W. D. Cooper (1844).

LETTERS, Selected and edited by R. B. Johnson (1927).

LETTERS, Edited by L. P. Curtis. Oxford (1935).
The standard edition.

Separate Works:

THE CASE OF ELIJAH. York (1747). *Sermon.*

THE ABUSES OF CONSCIENCE. York (1750). *Sermon.*

A POLITICAL ROMANCE [The History of a Good Warm Watch Coat]. York (1759). *Polemics.*

THE LIFE AND OPINIONS OF TRISTRAM SHANDY, 9 vols. (1759–67). *Novel.*
Popular current editions include those in Everyman's Library, the World's Classics, and Macdonald's Illustrated Classics.

A SENTIMENTAL JOURNEY THROUGH FRANCE AND ITALY, 2 vols. (1768). *Travel.*
Popular current editions include the Everyman's Library edition, with an introduction by G. Saintsbury, 1927, and the World's Classics editions with an introduction by V. Woolf, 1928. An edition with an introduction by H. Read appeared in 1929.

THE SECOND JOURNAL TO ELIZA, Edited by M. R. B. Shaw (1929).
The authenticity of this work is very doubtful.

Some Critical and Biographical Studies:

ILLUSTRATIONS OF STERNE, by J. Ferriar (1798).

MEMOIR OF STERNE, by W. Scott (1823).

LITERARY REMAINS, by S. T. Coleridge. Vol. i (1836).

THE ENGLISH HUMOURISTS, by W. M. Thackeray (1853).
Includes an unfavourable study of Sterne.

LIFE, by P. Fitzgerald. 2 vols. (1864).

LAURENCE STERNE, Sa Personne et ses Ouvrages, par P. Stapfer. Paris (1870).

HOURS IN A LIBRARY: III, by Leslie Stephen (1892).
Includes a critical study of Sterne.

STERNE, by H. D. Traill (1882).
In the English Men of Letters Series.

ESTIMATIONS IN CRITICISM, by W. Bagehot, Edited by C. Lennox (1909).
Includes a study 'Sterne and Thackeray'.

LIFE AND TIMES, by W. L. Cross, New York (1909).
  Important additions, 2 vols., New Haven, 1925; further revisions, New Haven 1929. This is the standard work on Sterne.
STERNE. A Study by W. Sichel (1910).
STERNE'S ELIZA, by A. Wright and W. L. Sclater (1923).
STERNE AND HIS NOVELS IN THE LIGHT OF MODERN PSYCHOLOGY, by A. Defroe. Groningen (1925).
  Despite its shortcomings, an interesting analysis.
THE ENGLISH COMIC CHARACTERS, by J. B. Priestley (1925).
  Includes 'The Brothers Shandy'.
THE POLITICKS OF LAURENCE STERNE, by L. P. Curtis, Oxford (1929).
THE SENSE OF GLORY, by R. Read (1931).
  Includes a study of Sterne.
THE COMMON READER: Second Series, by Virginia Woolf (1932).
  Contains an essay on *The Sentimental Journey; Sterne's Ghost* appears in *The Moment* by V. Woolf, 1947.
THE ENGLISH NOVELISTS, by A. Calder Marshall (1936).
  Includes a study of Sterne.
PHILOSOPHICAL INCURSIONS INTO ENGLISH LITERATURE, by J. Laird. Cambridge (1946).
  Includes 'Shandean Philosophy'.
THE UNSENTIMENTAL JOURNEY OF LAURENCE STERNE, by E. N. Dilworth. New York (1948).
  A study of Sterne's attitude to sentimentalism.
STERNE'S 'SERMONS OF MR. YORICK', by L. H. Hammond. New Haven (1948).
  Yale Studies in English, Vol. CVIII.
THE AGE OF JOHNSON. New Haven (1949).
  Includes 'Sterne: Apostle of Laughter', by R. D. F. Putney.
A STUDY OF THE WORD 'SENTIMENTAL', by E. Erämetsä. Helsinki (1951).
  Relevant to passages on p. 26 of this booklet.
TRISTRAM SHANDY'S WORLD. STERNE'S PHILOSOPHICAL RHETORIC, by John Traugott. University of California, Berkeley and Los Angeles (1954).
FROM DRYDEN TO JOHNSON, ed. Boris Ford (1957) (Pelican Guide to English Literature, Vol. 4).
  Includes '*Tristram Shandy* and its Tradition', by D. W. Jefferson.

WRITERS AND THEIR WORK

General Editor: BONAMY DOBRÉE

The first 55 issues in the Series appeared under the General Editorship of T. O. BEACHCROFT

Sixteenth Century and Earlier:
- CHAUCER: Nevill Coghill
- MALORY: M. C. Bradbrook
- MARLOWE: Philip Henderson
- SPENSER: Rosemary Freeman

Seventeenth Century:
- BUNYAN: Henri Talon
- DONNE: Frank Kermode
- DRYDEN: Bonamy Dobrée
- ANDREW MARVELL: John Press
- MILTON: E. M. W. Tillyard
- SHAKESPEARE: C. J. Sisson
- IZAAK WALTON: Margaret Bottrall

Eighteenth Century:
- BLAKE: Kathleen Raine
- BOSWELL: P. A. W. Collins
- BURKE: T. E. Utley
- BURNS: David Daiches
- CRABBE: R. L. Brett
- DEFOE: J. R. Sutherland
- FIELDING: John Butt
- GIBBON: C. V. Wedgwood
- GRAY: R. W. Ketton-Cremer
- JOHNSON: S. C. Roberts
- POPE: Ian Jack
- RICHARDSON: R. F. Brissenden
- SHERIDAN: W. A. Darlington
- SMOLLETT: Laurence Brander
- STERNE: D. W. Jefferson
- SWIFT: J. Middleton Murry
- HORACE WALPOLE: Hugh Honour

Nineteenth Century:
- MATTHEW ARNOLD: Kenneth Allott
- JANE AUSTEN: S. Townsend Warner
- THE BRONTË SISTERS: Phyllis Bentley
- SAMUEL BUTLER: G. D. H. Cole
- BYRON: Herbert Read
- CARLYLE: David Gascoyne
- LEWIS CARROLL: Derek Hudson
- COLERIDGE: Kathleen Raine
- DICKENS: K. J. Fielding
- GEORGE ELIOT: Lettice Cooper
- ENGLISH TRAVELLERS IN THE NEAR EAST: Robin Fedden
- THOMAS HARDY: R. A. Scott-James
- GERARD MANLEY HOPKINS: Geoffrey Grigson
- KEATS: Edmund Blunden
- LAMB: Edmund Blunden
- JOHN STUART MILL: Maurice Cranston
- WILLIAM MORRIS: Philip Henderson
- NEWMAN: J. M. Cameron
- ROSSETTI: O. Doughty
- RUSKIN: Peter Quennell
- SIR WALTER SCOTT: Ian Jack
- SHELLEY: Stephen Spender
- R. L. STEVENSON: G. B. Stern
- SWINBURNE: H. J. C. Grierson
- TENNYSON: F. L. Lucas
- OSCAR WILDE: James Laver
- WORDSWORTH: Helen Darbishire

Twentieth Century:
- W. H. AUDEN: Richard Hoggart
- HILAIRE BELLOC: Renée Haynes
- ARNOLD BENNETT: Frank Swinnerton
- EDMUND BLUNDEN: Alec M. Hardie
- ELIZABETH BOWEN: Jocelyn Brooke
- JOYCE CARY: Walter Allen

G. K. CHESTERTON:
 Christopher Hollis
WINSTON CHURCHILL:
 John Connell
R. G. COLLINGWOOD:
 E. W. F. Tomlin
I. COMPTON-BURNETT:
 Pamela Hansford Johnson
JOSEPH CONRAD: Oliver Warner
WALTER DE LA MARE:
 Kenneth Hopkins
NORMAN DOUGLAS: Ian Greenlees
T. S. ELIOT: M. C. Bradbrook
FORD MADOX FORD:
 Kenneth Young
E. M. FORSTER: Rex Warner
CHRISTOPHER FRY:
 Derek Stanford
JOHN GALSWORTHY:
 R. H. Mottram
ROBERT GRAVES:
 M. Seymour Smith
GRAHAM GREENE:
 Francis Wyndham
A. E. HOUSMAN: Ian Scott-Kilvert
ALDOUS HUXLEY: Jocelyn Brooke
HENRY JAMES: Michael Swan
JAMES JOYCE: J. I. M. Stewart
RUDYARD KIPLING:
 Bonamy Dobrée
D. H. LAWRENCE: Kenneth Young
C. DAY LEWIS: Clifford Dyment

WYNDHAM LEWIS:
 E. W. F. To
KATHERINE MANSFIELD:
 Ian Gor
JOHN MASEFIELD: L. A. G. Stro
SOMERSET MAUGHAM:
 John Bro
EDWIN MUIR: J. C. Hall
J. MIDDLETON MURRY:
 Philip M
GEORGE ORWELL: Tom Hopkir
J. B. PRIESTLEY: Ivor Brown
HERBERT READ: Francis Berry
BERTRAND RUSSELL:
 Alan Dorv
BERNARD SHAW: A. C. Ward
EDITH SITWELL: John Lehmann
OSBERT SITWELL: Roger Fulfor
LYTTON STRACHEY:
 R. A. Scott-Ja
DYLAN THOMAS: G. S. Fraser
G. M. TREVELYAN: J. H. Plumb
WAR POETS 1914–18:
 Edmund Blun
EVELYN WAUGH:
 Christopher H
H. G. WELLS: Montgomery Belgi
CHARLES WILLIAMS:
 John Heath-St
VIRGINIA WOOLF:
 Bernard Blackst
W. B. YEATS: G. S. Fraser

In Preparation:

Sixteenth Century and Earlier:
ENGLISH MARITIME WRITING:
HAKLUYT TO COOK:
 Oliver Warner

Seventeenth Century:
SIR THOMAS BROWNE:
 Peter Green

Eighteenth Century:
STEELE, ADDISON & TH
 PERIODICAL ESSAYS:
 A. R. Humph
GOLDSMITH: A. Norman Jeffares

Nineteenth Century:
BROWNING: John Bryson
GISSING: A. C. Ward
THACKERAY: Laurence Brander